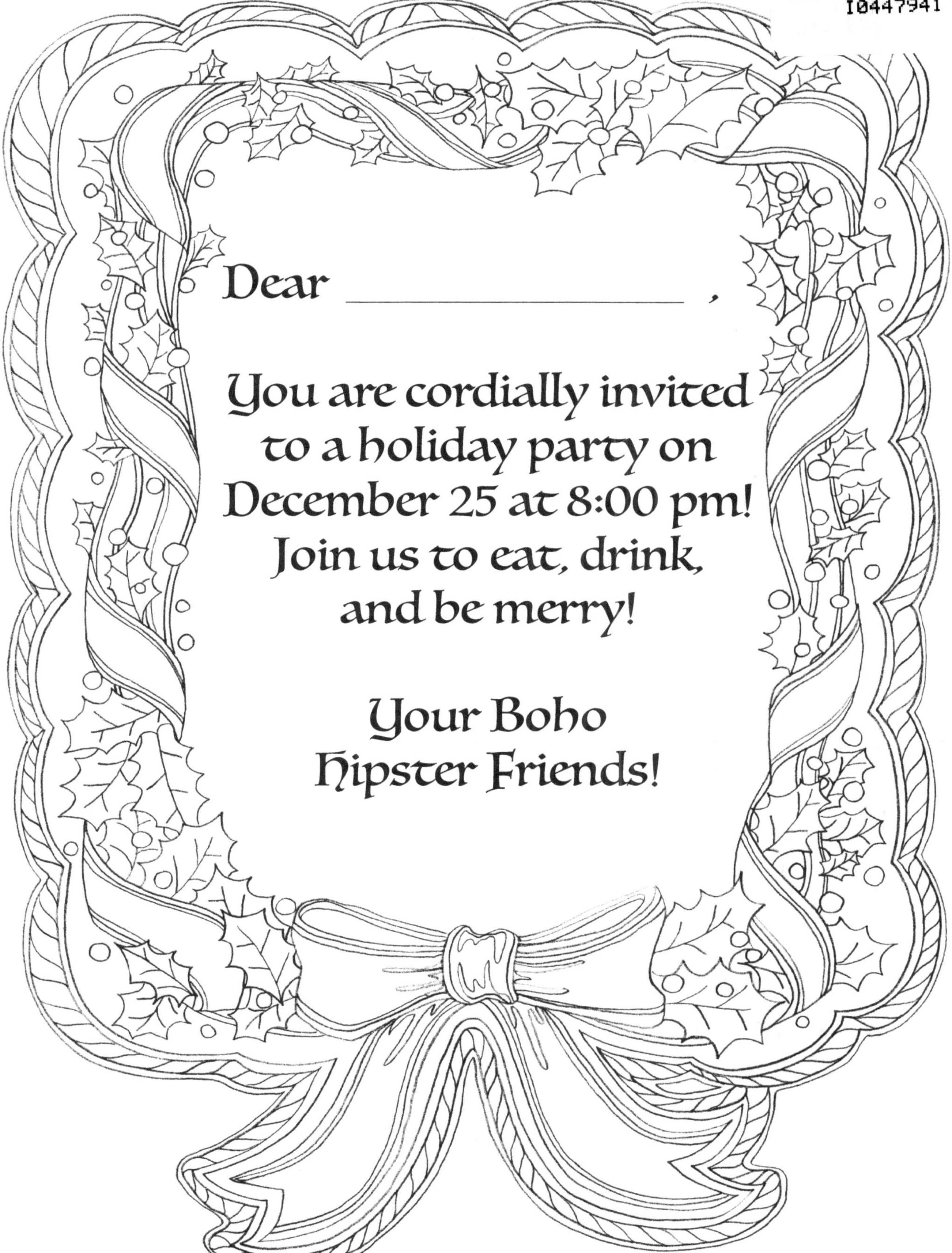
Dear ____________________ ,
You are cordially invited
to a holiday party on
December 25 at 8:00 pm!
Join us to eat, drink,
and be merry!
Your Boho
Hipster Friends!

Boho Hipster

Happy Holiday

Sandy Mahony
Mary Lou Brown

Hello
Winter

Merry
Christmas

xmas

Grab your coffee
I ♥ Holidays
cozy
mug ♥

Grab your coffee
I ♥ Holidays
Cozy
Winter
mug ♥
its time to read a good book
Warm Hugs
Hello

Merry Christmas

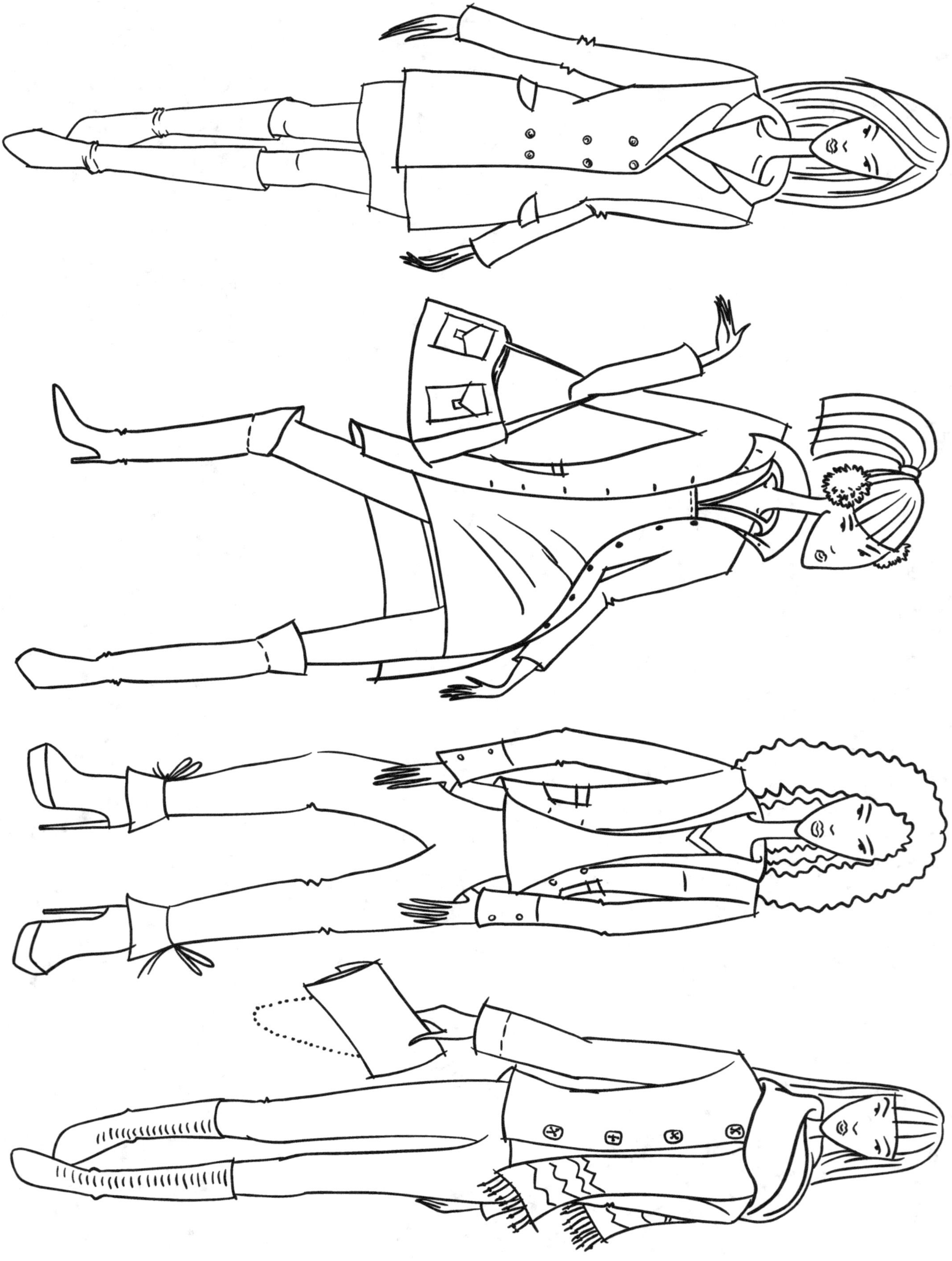

adventurelearningpress.com

www.ingramcontent.com/pod-product-compliance
Lightning Source LLC
Chambersburg PA
CBHW081330310526
45789CB00018B/2998